Memory's Abacus

Memory's Abacus

POEMS

Anna Lewis

WISEBLOOD BOOKS

2024

WISEBLOOD BOOKS
Post Office Box 870
Menomonee Falls, Wisconsin 53052

PRINTED IN THE UNITED STATES OF AMERICA
Cover design by Kristen Ponak & Amanda Brown
Typesetting by Terrence Chouinard

ISBN: 978-1-951319-01-4

to my parents
Gavin Lewis & Nadezhda Katyk-Lewis

to my brothers & sister
Michael, Alexander, & Dorothea

Memory's Abacus

WINNOWER OF WHEAT TO THE WINDS

translation from the French of Joachim du Bellay

To you, light troop,
who softly swoop
past all this world
on transient wings
and set astir
shade and green burgeonings,

I bring violets,
lilies, a riot
of buds, carnations,
and this token,
red oblation:
roses, just now open.

May your cool breath
this field refresh
and quicken time.
I winnow wheat—
such a great climb
for my breath in this heat.

I

ABOVE IT

It's not that I don't know it when I'm in it,
searching for a spot to park my liquid
assets or, faster than a New York minute,
remit them into gritty circulation,
while heels and tires haul their various
freight around for public estimated valuation.

It's just that, as the plane gains height and veers
first left, then right, I hear some inner guide indicate
the topography: Atlantic Ocean, here;
Ellis Island, that splotch down there, see?
Observe the mighty grid. (It looks like a grid.)
East River; Hudson; bridges—one, two, three—

Mid-air and miles above the hand-over-fist,
it strikes me: that's our soul. We do exist.

DISAPPEARING ACT

You wheel against the churning of the sky,
enveloped by the brightness of the sun,
as if you've found your mother's face again,
the way she beamed when she was young.

Euphoria insists on greater heights
so on you fly, and up, and higher still,
until your father seems a tiny bird
at play among the ocean's silken hills.

And then: the scent of prayer from molten wax,
a whir of feathers all about you blown,
your body baked and solid as a stone,
and you are no one.

Sky, above.
Below, the foam.

APRIL FUNERAL

At noon, our family forms a small parade.
We pass a line of cherry trees in white,
a fragile wall against your cruel charade
of summer bluffed by rays too hot, too bright.

Once at the grave, no charity of shade.
Just broad resoundings. Three successive booms
advancing in salute. Your very light
appears to hold aloft our moans. The bloom

of "Taps," reminding us of dusk, incites
still more, it seems, your gleam, your callous loom.
Too soon, your pressing heat, our home unmade.
Like bones, our closest words and customs strewn.

Outrageous, your ubiquitous cascade.
Beyond belief, your absence from his tomb.

MEMORY'S ABACUS

No
siblings.
Ten cousins
once, though. *Loren.*
Elizabeth. Our
grandmother taps on the
Christmas tablecloth as if
there lay memory's abacus.
Ernie. Harley. Mabel. Bill. Just two
doors down, she adds, *always in a jumble.*
Dispersed now or dead, her childhood kin
reunite as a line of names
along her swollen knuckles.
For each she accounts with-
in the span of her
grasp. *Louellen.*
Jane. Mary
Margaret.
May.

THE STORM

And see, it's stopping now, she said, *so*
back to work with you, it wasn't much.
The boy hung round her skirts. *That depends,*
he thought, *on how you measure.* Upon
the kitchen table lay nine eggs, a
bounty he had gathered from the red
coop just when, rumbling like the old wheel
of a weary, indifferent barrow,
clouds had come, poured forth their load, and glazed
the coop, the boy, the eggs, all things, with
a new and glistening skin of rain.
If, the boy thought further, *the water*
can be measured. He stood now beside
the door and opened it: to test the
air, which hung sopping; to scan the white
sky and, as they emerged, the chickens.

CHILDHOOD HOME

Hamilton, New Jersey

The house on Redwood Avenue
was full of stairs and doors.
The curtains tossed forth promises.
We voyaged through old drawers.

The garden breezed with irises
and, on the laundry line,
our dresses dried in time for church
and Sunday lunch and wine.

Each blossom on the dogwood tree
would open like a book.
Our Babinka would tug a branch
down close to give a look:

the rusty stains at petal's edge
denoted holy wounds;
the bristling core, a crown of thorns;
the Passion in a bloom.

And—fragile hope—the balcony
we always wished to build
still seems to overhang somewhere
like prayer gone unfulfilled.

PERSEPHONE CALLS HOME

When I was small, I'd lean in close to you
and talk away as if some inner dam
had somehow burst so, like a brilliant blue
cascade of water, words rushed forth to slam

their happy way into the ample flow
of your words, winding like a white river
below, beginning to bulge and billow
over, white and blue becoming silver

tide, but now we mainly speak on the phone.
Our words are few and tight, of little worth.
Each thin exchange reminds me I'm alone.
Each paltry effort indicates a dearth.

I've grown. I think you've grown. Yet how we speak
has dwindled from a torrent to a leak.

ARACHNE

For each of us,
a time arrives
of spindled limbs;
of lusts like knives;

of weaving ways
with gossamer smirks
away from home,
from gods; of work

adored, begrudged;
of reins we clasp
in naked hands;
of dangled gasps;

of fine suspension;
of gauzy aches;
of trembling webs
our own to make.

RAILWAY LINE, WINDOW SEAT

There's nothing to be seen along the track
unless you count the endless piles of junk,
deranged as if by some colossal drunk;
the plenitude of filth; the heft of lack;

the silhouettes of trees on sodden walls,
on balconies that rage with plastic toys;
the shadow of a blossom crisply poised
across a dumbstruck face that is a doll's.

PLOTLINES

When young, we learn what should come first and next.
We plot our course on some imagined chart,
expecting things to be what we expect.

Beginning seems a cinch in some respects.
It's *once upon a time* where we all start.
So young we learn what should come first and next.

But putting shoes and socks on proves complex,
a topsy-turvy, labyrinthine art.
The unexpected's what we least expect.

Then getting somewhere seems forever hexed.
The silly horse will trail the silly cart,
despite our knowing what comes first and next.

The latter standard sequencing neglects
of which the former's, well, parcel and part.
See? Nothing's what they say the blessed expect.

Beware. The plot's most likely to perplex
there where it touches matters of the heart.
We were young and cursèd. Our first and next
expected somethings? Just as you'd expect.

STUDY IN WHITE

A gull hovers,
expands its wings.
Fullness, brightness,
Easter hymns.

A linen sheet
churns the air
upon a line.
Billowed prayer.

Along the tracks,
a pallid shawl.
Lamb astray,
plaintive call.

From mothers'
lips, soft unfurl
lies. Sweet milk.
Beads of pearl.

BROKEN SONNET

I dropped it last July but still I keep
our rosy porcelain bowl, a small collection
of jagged shards arranged into a heap.
I've found debris can serve up recollection

of breakfast peach; of honey milk at night;
the breath of steam, its yearning for your face;
the darkest queues our bodies would recite
to one another; lines they would retrace.

And now, outside, October sweeps the stones,
shells, sand, bits of shattered leaf with keen gusts.
And still I can't discard these simple bones
of clay and glaze.
                    And still I can't relinquish them to dust.

ECHO LAKE

I wake and hear the mourning dove again,
his calling for the mate who's gone away
to make her home elsewhere along the lake.

I picture, from my sheets, the tranquil lake
rippled by his calls—again and again,
they send themselves aloft and draw away

perhaps just as our losses find a way
to crease, leave off, re-crease the mountain-lake-
like stillness held by selves we soothe again.

Again, day smoothes its way along the lake.

FIGMENT OF IMAGINATION

The evidence
now overwhelms:
your tugging thirst,
your thousand realms

of hunger, each
so deep and wild,
there's no question.
I'm with child.

Exponential
growth from nothing,
still unseen,
unheard, yet something

urges me
to eat our fill,
to slow my pace
and sleep until

a kick
inside somewhere
jolts me awake—
who's there?

PASSERSBY

Hello, beautiful,
said the homeless man,
and what could she do—

tired, as usual;
almost immovable;
emotions, to say the least,
highly mutable;
pregnancy, by then,
roundly indisputable;
belly, at that point,
a corpulent crucible—

but say
thank you.

WHAT ELSE IS THERE

between the landing
and the stair;

within thin cups
reposed on saucers;

after we have tidied up;
before we linger

in the hall;
beyond our finger

tips, like matches
missed; or, once we've burned

first, bitter batches—
what else have we

as sky leans in
to grace our trees

and sooner gives
itself to later—but this

one life that's more,
almost, than we can bear?

II

REVERIES OF A MOTHER ON FOOT

Durham, North Carolina · for Kolya

1

Your sleeping face brims wide as paradise.
Magnolia branches, freshly budding, lace.
The stroller glides. I make my steps precise.
Your sleeping face brims wide as paradise.
Beneath our humid, morning sky, I splice
motherhood and solitude without a trace.
Your sleeping face brims wide as paradise.
Magnolia branches, freshly budding, lace.

2

Magnolia branches bud. Babinka's lace.
Body and blood of ours, swaddled in sleep.
Your breathing measures out a steady pace.
Magnolia branches bud. Babinka's lace.
Sweet boy, I watch the lushness of your face.
Sacred sleep. *While o'er thee thy mother weep.*
Magnolia branches bud. Babinka's lace.
Body and blood of ours, swaddled in sleep.

3

Body and blood of ours, swaddled in sleep.
To think you won't remember this at all.
Our journeyings and dreams aren't ours to keep.
Moments, minutes, hours, swaddled in sleep.
A puddle glimmers: mirror-fair, sky-deep.
When the bough breaks, the cradle will fall.
Body and blood of ours, swaddled in sleep.
To think you won't remember this at all.

4

Or *when* will you remember this at all?
It takes some time to start to build a past,
to sense and save and sift; one day, recall:
the kitchen table, when remembering was all
we did; Maminka's bread; her woolen shawl.
You twist. An eyelid flits—awake at last!
I know you won't remember this at all.
It takes some time to start to build a past.

5

And yet, somehow, we start to build a past.
We learn the world in mirrored syllables.
Green, I prompt. You venture, *geen!* Beads of glass.
It takes some time to start to build a past.
Green—geen! Grass—gass! Our broadcast
doubles what's becoming visible.
It takes some time to start to build a past.
We learn the world in mirrored syllables.

6

We sing our song of mirrored syllables.
Each slip of sound invites its twin to play.
Our echoing proves irresistible.
We sing our song of mirrored syllables
as if we might unriddle some riddle
of sound and sense as old and deep as clay.
We cast the world in mirrored syllables.
Each slip of sound invites its twin to play.

7

A slip of sound invites its twin to play.
I recollect the girl I used to be.
She kept her longings neatly tucked away.
A slip of sound invites its twin to play.
Her heart held onto things too hard: the day,
the way the light lit up our dogwood tree.
A slip of sound invites its twin to play.
A hint of me, the girl I used to be.

8

A hint of me, the girl I used to be.
She had a way of always glancing back
within her heart to glimpse our family tree.
A hint of me, the girl I used to be,
in search of faces she would never see.
She snipped her steps, avoiding every crack.
A hint of me, the girl I used to be,
still here, still walking forward, glancing back.

9

Still here, still walking forward, glancing back,
still finding walking is a way of dreaming,
of wandering into memory's hidden tracks.
Still here, still walking forward, glancing back.
Somewhere, a mourner's freshly dressed in black.
Ahead, a bowl of lentil soup was steaming
as I walked forward, home, while glancing back.
Already, walking was a way of dreaming.

10

Already, walking was a way of dreaming,
an airy scheming between earth and sky.
(Perhaps it's all to keep from screaming.)
Already, walking was a way of dreaming,
each crisply measured step redeeming
the day, a word, a gesture gone awry.
Already, walking was a way of dreaming,
an airy scheming between earth and sky.

11

An airy scheming between earth and sky
awakens voices buried long ago.
I overhear Babinka weep goodbye.
An airy scheming between earth and sky
revives an unremembered lullaby,
a tone, a tongue we never quite outgrow.
An airy scheming between earth and sky
awakens voices buried long ago.

12

The phone! A voice! A friend from long ago
reports her father's death. Absorb the sting.
She wished to bridge the time and let me know.
The phone! A voice—a friend's from long ago
has winged into our blooming air. We slow.
Your mellow eyes hold mine. A blossom swings.
The phone! A voice! A friend from long ago
reports her father's death. Absorb the sting.

13

Report: Grandfather's death. Absorb the sting
as, still, the door insists on being opened
when bills and boxes make the doorbell ring.
Report: Grandfather's death. Absorb the sting.
Our unrelenting journey still will bring
its tedious rhythm, its tireless motion.
Report: Grandfather's death. Absorb the sting
as, still, the door insists on being opened.

14

I knew which drawer; it had to be opened
to light a candle for Grandfather's death.
The house was dark; our thoughts unspoken.
I knew which drawer; it had to be opened
and one unbroken candle chosen
to gasp with flame, to take a breath.
I knew which drawer; it had to be opened
to light a candle for Grandfather's death.

15

We light a candle for Grandfather's death.
Not for the first time, I see him in you.
The ache, however nursed, will ache afresh.
We light a candle for Grandfather's death.
Time and tide prove even tiny you his flesh
and blood each passing day more than I knew.
We light a candle for Grandfather's death.
Not for the first time, I see him in you.

16

Not for the first time, I see him in you.
There's an ache and some solace in seeing
a face within a face, his image peering through.
Not for the first time I see him in you:
a way, a gleam, made miniscule and new.
More proof there's no such thing as fleeing.
Not for the first time, I see him in you.
There's an ache and some solace in seeing.

17

There's an ache and some solace in being
neither here nor there but on our way.
A daily journey, even, can be freeing.
There's an ache and some solace in being
in-between; it feels something like believing.
A daily route grows newer by the day.
There's an ache and some solace in being
neither here nor there but on our way.

18

We're neither here nor there but on our way.
Inside, our tasks unattended to, bide.
Discord. Doors slam. What else is there to say?
We're neither here nor there but on our way.
The open air does wonders to allay
the flare of rage, the sightless grip of pride.
We're neither here nor there but on our way.
Inside, our tasks unattended to, bide.

19

Inside, our tasks unattended to, bide:
the disaster kitchen; the naked bed;
the endless debris of our homespun tide.
Inside, our tasks unattended to, bide,
try though we may to catch up, get ahead.
The hours run off like a stolen bride.
Inside, our tasks unattended to, bide:
the disaster kitchen; the naked bed.

20

The disaster kitchen, the naked bed
bear too many stains, too long ignored.
Defiled pillows cradle our heads.
The disaster kitchen, the naked bed,
the accusations that remain unsaid
but dangle overhead like broken cords.
The disaster kitchen, the naked bed
bear too many stains, too long ignored.

21

Too many stains, too long ignored.
No getting them out till the end of our days.
Our string of abuses, carefully scored.
Too many stains, too long ignored.
The invisible ink of slights that we hoard
to savor in later peaks of malaise.
Too many stains, too long ignored.
No getting them out till the end of our days.

22

There's no moving out till the end of our days.
We go back to each corner, still listening for clues.
The creak of a new door recalls some old phrase.
There's no moving out till the end of our days.
New walls make of voices the same tonal haze
of meaning we'd bend to, from the stairs, then lose.
There's no moving out till the end of our days.
We go back to each corner, still listening for clues.

23

I go back to each corner, still listening for clues
even now as my face undeniably falls
like old glass in a pane. Ripples accrue.
I go back to each corner still listening for clues.
Our lullabies hide and reveal what's true.
Down will come baby, cradle and all.
I go back to each corner, still listening for clues,
even now, as my face undeniably falls.

24

It's true. My face undeniably falls.
It's plain as plain can be in the mirror,
where everything's backward except time's crawl.
It's true. My face undeniably falls.
One glimpse and I halt to read new scrawls
around my eyes. There must be some error.
But it's true. My face undeniably falls.
It's plain as plain can be in the mirror.

25

Last night, awake, we gazed in the mirror.
A moon, you announced and, pointing, chirped, *up.*
Recast in the glass, the moon hung nearer.
Last night, awake, we gazed in the mirror.
A reflection, reflected: she almost shone clearer
and, eye to eye almost, perhaps I feared her.
Awake, together, we gazed in the mirror.
A moon, you announced and, pointing, chirped, *up.*

26

A moon, you announced and, pointing, chirped, *up.*
No teaching you, yet, what makes it *the* moon,
how, night after night, things can really add up.
A moon, you announced and, pointing, chirped, *up.*
Why argue that this and last night's match up
with each other, tomorrow's—that none of it's new?
A moon, you announced and, pointing, chirped, *up.*
No teaching you, yet, what makes it *the* moon.

27

No teaching you yet what makes it the moon,
that we walk to the grave, that each grave is a door,
how ages and ages from now is too soon.
No teaching you yet what makes it the moon,
how midnight's the secret lover of noon.
One day, in your heart, you'll hear the sea roar.
No teaching you yet what makes it the moon,
that we walk to the grave, that each grave is a door.

28

We walk to the grave. Each grave is a door.
Our afternoon sky hangs bright as a page.
Listen: in our hearts, we hear the sea roar.
We walk to the grave. Each grave is a door.
You'll always be mine, all mothers have sworn.
Listen: in our hearts, we hear the sea rage.
We walk to the grave. Each grave is a door.
Our afternoon sky hangs bright as a page.

29

Our afternoon sky hangs bright as a page.
There is war in my home, so I seek a new home
wept a voice via radio; kitchen outrage.
Our afternoon sky hangs bright as a page.
Somewhere, there's despair that I can't assuage
from my opposite end of our whispering dome.
Our afternoon sky hangs bright as a page.
There is war in my home, so I seek a new home.

30

There is war in my home, so I seek a new home.
I try to imagine some kind of straight line
from here to the mother who desperately roams.
There is war in my home, so I seek a new home.
Does it help that I care? Between us wind rhizomes
of borders, orders, disorder, landmines.
There is war in my home, so I seek a new home.
I try to imagine some kind of straight line.

31

I try to imagine some kind of straight line,
as if to hang all the world from a rope.
But the pavement twists like a leafless vine.
I try to imagine some kind of straight line
but even the good streets, watched by benign
verandas, unevenly crumble and slope.
I try to imagine some kind of straight line,
as if to hang all the world from a rope.

32

If I could hang all the world from a rope,
would the winds be kind to the rough stretch on Green,
its cinderblock homes, peeling and piss-soaked?
If I could hang all the world from a rope,
would I air my shame when the poor kids lope
close to the stroller in thin, filthy jeans?
If I could hang all the world from a rope,
would the winds be kind to the rough stretch on Green?

33

Nobody's kind to the rough stretch on Green,
between the creek and the broad empty road.
I admit it: I hurry, hoping not to be seen.
Nobody's kind to the rough stretch on Green.
If I quicken my stride, what does that mean?
Do pace and footfall send a coward's code?
Nobody's kind to the rough stretch on Green,
between the creek and the broad empty road.

34

Between the creek and the broad empty road,
I wonder about our final walk home.
I quicken my strides and lean into my load.
Between the creek and the broad empty road,
your eyes, sweet boy, have wondrously closed.
Each of us slowly turns clay into loam.
Between the creek and the broad empty road,
I wonder about our final walk home.

35

What grace shall we know in our final walk home—
quick collapse, or the slow-sinking days of dementia,
or a heinous descent from sky to sea foam?
What grace shall we know in our final walk home
who, spurning doubt, in joyful hope, still comb
the seen and unseen to find new dimensions?
What grace shall we know in our final walk home—
quick collapse, or the slow-sinking days of dementia?

36

You visit the slow-sinking, dazed by dementia.
You offer your hand. They hold on fast and tight.
You're struck by the folly of good intentions.
You visit the slow-sinking, dazed by dementia.
There's little to give or to gain of redemption.
You offer your hand. Theirs is so light.
You visit the slow-sinking, dazed by dementia.
You offer your hand. They hold on fast and tight.

37

But don't we all hold on so fast and tight
that what we find impossible to grasp
is how to let things go, leave, disunite,
preferring to hold on so fast and tight
that, day after day and night after night,
the very thought of loosening our clasp—
I'll just keep holding on so fast and tight!—
itself becomes impossible to grasp?

38

The thought of letting go is hard to grasp.
What does it take, in fact, to slip away,
the air between us sudden as a gasp?
The thought of letting go is hard to grasp.
Now daylight's loosening; the stroller rasps.
Magnolias breathe—so what if I delay?
The thought of letting go is hard to grasp.
What does it take, in fact, to slip away?

39

The fading daylight's soon to slip away.
The gentle sparrows rise and disappear.
Heads bowed, the Lenten roses seem to pray.
The fading daylight's soon to slip away.
Our sky transforms from dove to charcoal gray,
the moon half-hidden now, a tarnished sphere.
The fading daylight's soon to slip away.
The gentle sparrows rise and disappear.

40

The gentle sparrows rise and disappear.
Your sleeping face brims wide as paradise.
We're almost home; the end is very near.
The gentle sparrows rise and disappear.
It's time my heart admit our passing here
in quivering air: This must suffice.
The gentle sparrows rise and disappear.
Your sleeping face brims wide as paradise.

III

MORNING DROP-OFF

Durham, North Carolina

Early light cuts sharp against brick walls.
Already hot, this little town breathes hard.
Cars pass. We pause. *Can you say car?*
But words are just beyond your tender grasp.

Here, along the dusty road, an old
magnolia swaddles new, white petals
into buds, each as quiet as an egg.
Cars pause. We pass. The traffic thickens soon

as morning swells against the edge of day.
Great ventilators buzz from City Hall.
Already, babies bleat and clomp upon
the daycare's polygon of scraggy grass.

Almost, your heart and mine have learned to part.
I loose you from my arms and move away.

ON SEEING HOPPER'S *ROOMS BY THE SEA* WITH A FRIEND

Between inside and out, a cool, gray wall.
A trapezoid of light through open door.
A settee, red. A carpet, green. The hall,
a yellow passage not to sandy shore
but hard to some blue sea below. That's all.
No action here. Just color, shape, and light.
No saints in gold-leaf haloes to adore.
But, as you almost pass it, left to right,
I see you pause before its either/or:
the calm suspension, here, right now, of white,
as light through cool, gray rooms conducts its fall;
or there, beyond, a square of blue, the sight
of lustrous sky and ocean. Still, you stall.
You stand before the brink, its unseen height.

SOLSTITIUM

The only sound was cormorant clatter
across the heat and the sea's coral hills.
Silent as mangroves, you and I paddled.
It seemed to me, love, that the sun stood still.

That was Key West. Now I'm back in Brooklyn.
You've migrated someplace I've never seen.
The copper sun slots itself down Union,
varnishing brick with an igneous sheen.

I aim my phone at city-squeezed radiance.
Where you are, you'll hear a digital chirp,
the song of our long-distance alliance,
launched across networks to you on some perch:

I send the sun via handheld device—
or almost—these pixels, inert as ice.

HEARTBREAK

Who's to say
if it flakes; or sinks from a throne;
how the ache
steals in to feast on muscle tone;

if its burst
yields a soapy, prismatic pop;
which is worse—
the thunderous flutter or the stop;

if it blackens
like magic or winks like smashed glass;
what happens,
just then, to its center of mass;

by what flame
some good nurse tries to darn the hole;
from what flame
you will birth—agony!—your new soul.

MIGRAINE WITH AURA

Have at my
cerebral soil.
Here I am.
Come. Uncoil

your secret sprout,
curious offspring,
spawn obscure—
there's not a thing

could oust you
from your lurk
among synapses
gone berserk

and cranial nerves
you set on fire,
pleased among
their seething briars.

Softly spread,
exquisite bloom,
as I withdraw
to a darkened room,

surrendering
my day. It's fine.
You steal but
also gift me time

for solitude.
Shimmer there
beyond my grasp
in glassy air.

MISS SCARLET, IN THE STUDY, WITH A SCUPPERNONG

Globe of bronze,
your bitter sheath
splits and spawns
ambrosial flesh,

and I'm refreshed.
It's almost dawn.
I slip asleep,
hot care withdrawn.

ROOM: VARIATION ON A DEFINITION

A measure of space tending towards romance:
my rogue it is comes catches me up in
a romp or romps, hence renders a cottage
a tower, some linen, a fine bed of coal;
producing a roof or a canopy
often denoting the summit of something
derived or descended from fire, from gypsies,
from successions of stars, from the power
of moving; as in a river to a castle
or a heaven to a hovel; makes way;
yields place; urges to flight; causes to resound
this particular portion of space or a spot
esp. a garden, a perfume, the swell of
a choir, a sun, or, by extension, a sky.

HOME, WINDOW SEAT

I'm sure I'd go mad,
were this all I had.

But, still, to come home
and be quite alone

for a spell before
you come through the door

(well believing you will)
while, upon the sill,

the last line of sun
delays, not yet done,

and draws the cat
to its glow—all this *this*

isn't *that,*
but it's *this* nonetheless.

SEE?

In the end, it was our bed sheets on the line—

the hanging of which
in this day and age
the merits of which
we'd long debated—

that made us fly out-of-doors just in time

to become the quiet before the storm
in witness of the first, fat droplets being born.

EASTER RIVER

Our Easter afternoon already warm
enough to bring to mind our river spot
where we'd come again to find our way
along our forest path that whispers, true,

with highway sound but also has our swing,
the vine that swayed with both our weights, and crawls
with oakworms we would try to count and bends
to give a sudden view of current, dark

as wine and sparkling with the day—all just as
we'd left it—here I stagger over boulders
at the sight of shoulders, bare and broader now—
yours!—even as you spring in boyish play.

Our waters test how well love has me know
and not know you, thus baring you anew.

NARCISSUS ONLINE

Friend, time was we were palms upon
palms in the clapping air and *click*
was the flick of a switch elsewhere.

Sto, stare, steti, statum, step
into the same river. A swarm
of updates fragile as notes left

for the dead or Echo's replies:
Here! Come! Have me! Stay! Here! Come! Have—
Look. Like. Link. River to stream, stream

to sky, bead to bead to measure
a prayer. Ripple to ripple, page
to page with a digital hinge.

Friend, book, face more beheld, face more
upheld than all divinities,
beyond or behind, wend your way

from gleam to gleam. To aqua glare
fixate your liked and liking stare.

TO EURYDICE

Because the bitter root of doubt entwined
me from the first as you and I stumbled
through the dark because my song seemed not

enough because I knew I'd charmed my way
into the depths, into a set of bloodless terms
because to charm is not to guide is not

to trust because the slightest line of sun
ahead sufficed to make me feel again
undone and human in my need to see

with my own eyes your face, I did. I did look back.

AS EVERY FALL

The leaves had blanketed without a sound
the earth, a damp and chilly vault by then,
when she and I together knelt again,
as every fall, to place you in the ground

and plotted, all the while, how you would spring:
your nip of green at play in dewy air;
your mop of leaves, a thick, unkempt affair;
your bud, a bird preparing to take wing—

as if to bloom is not to come undone,
each petal's hinge unhinging in the light
and loosening itself from something tight,
each flake of color dropping once unspun—

as if your beauty weren't in your collapse,
in how you blaze as back to earth you lapse.

CEMETERY VISIT

for my father

And here we are again, before your name
engraved in simple letters on this stone,
these markings we have known since early days—
arranged across the lines of every form,
on envelopes, in print or shaped by hand,
on all our fluttering, pink permission slips,
on checks financed by hours at your desk
and tendered to us as gifts to ease our way,
on books you wrote we only somewhat read
to which we now return in search of more—

just so, your letters in their self-same row

except that here where, rooted in an earth
that reels and quivers, still, *roses, crocus,*
beautiful violets, iris blossoms too,
and hyacinth spread their sweet fragrance,
where pressing sunlight warms each letter's path,
your name's expression, from within this face
of granite, meets and holds our eyes that scanned,
with every step, the quiet, windworn crowd,
and seems almost to more than name you now.
We greet your name and wait for greeting back.

SEASCAPE

As if you've disappeared at sea,

I turn to scan the lines of surf and sky
and think back on those years which seem

to tumble from my hands like shells
we'd walked along the tide to glean—

each luminescent in its blues or grays,
or with a miracle of finely penciled rows

that round, in pink, a corrugated curve,
or with a shimmer of silver that shows

when wet with brine, quick shard of mirror—
and which I work to restore to my keeping,

all the while believing that this great expanse
we used to view together from right here

(I know it as our own the way one knows
a stretch of sand however it may shift)

and which now swells as if between us, lengthens
when, if anything, it shortens:

it's I who journeys on to come ashore to you.

A GHAZAL FOR WET DAYS

Lo, the wind and the rain.
Oh, the wind and the rain.

Endless spin of a skein—
so the wind and the rain.

Blithely, rows of complaint
sow the wind and the rain.

I begin to make gains—
no—the wind and the rain.

Nameless forests and plains
know this wind and this rain.

Wild within, undetained,
flow the wind and the rain.

Your prim trimming's in vain,
crow the wind and the rain.

Wet and woeful refrain—
Hey, ho, the wind and the rain.

Oh, to end in my name.
No, go the wind and the rain.

I AM GRATEFUL to the editors of the following publications, where some of these poems first appeared, sometimes in slightly different form:

Atticus Review: "Solstitium"
The Evansville Review: "Disappearing Act"
First Things: "Above It"
MEASURE: A Review of Formal Poetry: "Morning Drop-Off"
Modern Age: A Conservative Review: "As Every Fall;" "On Seeing Hopper's
   Rooms *By The Sea* with a Friend"
The Raintown Review: "Study In White"
THINK: A Journal of Poetry, Fiction, and Essays: "A Ghazal for Wet Days"
Valparaiso Poetry Review: "What Else Is There"

I owe thanks to many: to the professors who guided my literary development, especially William C. Dowling; to Susannah Hollister, Erica McAlpine, and Siobhan Phillips for their example and kindness; to Judy Rowe Michaels, who was first in growing me as a writer; and with special gratitude to Rachel Hadas for her generous mentorship.

I am indebted to James Matthew Wilson for his critical guidance and encouragement as I sought to publish this work. Micah Mattix too gave vital encouragement. Joanna Penn Cooper shared helpful insight, and Ron Starbuck has been a gracious supporter. My deepest thanks to Joshua Hren and Mary Finnegan of Wiseblood Books for bringing this work to life with such care and commitment.

Along the way, friends have buoyed and inspired more than they know: Emily Bloom, Marguerita de Senna, Gerri Houlihan and the dancers of The Big Red Dance Project, Liz Hall, K-Sue Park, Trey Sartin, Jen Snow.

Above all, I'm grateful to my family. I thank Nicole and Kolya for the loving home life in which I wrote these poems. I thank and dedicate this book to my parents and to Michael, Sash, and Dolly who, together, shaped the early life in which it has its roots.

ANNA LEWIS was born and raised in New Jersey. She studied literature at Rutgers, the Sorbonne, and Yale. Her essays and poems have appeared in *Modern Age: A Conservative Review, Yale Review Online, The Washington Post, First Things, MEASURE,* and elsewhere. She works in the technology industry and lives in Durham, North Carolina with her husband and son. *Memory's Abacus* is her first book.

Printed in the USA
CPSIA information can be obtained
at www.ICGtesting.com
JSHW011716080224
56838JS00007B/195

9 781951 319014